PRAY WITHOUT CEASING

THIRTY-ONE DAYS IN PRAYER

AUDREY TOUSANT SHELBY, MSW

WESTBOW
PRESS®
A DIVISION OF THOMAS NELSON
& ZONDERVAN

Illustrations by: Wendy R of pandyartwalk, Digital Illustrator

WestBow Press books may be ordered through booksellers or by contacting:

WestBow Press
A Division of Thomas Nelson & Zondervan
1663 Liberty Drive
Bloomington, IN 47403
www.westbowpress.com
844-714-3454

ISBN: 979-8-3850-2261-8 (sc)
ISBN: 979-8-3850-2262-5 (hc)
ISBN: 979-8-3850-2263-2 (e)

Library of Congress Control Number: 2024906462

Print information available on the last page.

WestBow Press rev. date: 05/16/2024

To my family

I prayed for someone to love, and God gave me you. Always know that when you pray, God hears you. I love you.

INTRODUCTION

Pray without ceasing.

—1 Thessalonians 5:17 (ESV)

While journaling and praying one morning, I heard a soft voice say, "Write a book about prayer." I quickly jotted that down. Then I heard, "Pray without ceasing." I wrote that down too. What I heard is often called a small voice, or people like to say, "Something told me." I was sure that I heard God.

I should have known that when God told me to write a book about prayer, I would go through situations that require prayer. I have gone through various trials since starting this book in late 2022. I have had serious family conflicts. I have experienced health challenges, and my husband was diagnosed with colon cancer. Through it all, I still put my faith in God. I hope this book will inspire you to hope again … one prayer at a time.

Pray without Ceasing encourages you to reflect on your own journey as you peak into the experiences of the author. Each day provides a journal prompt and a prayer section, inspiring deeper reflection. Rounding out each day are beautifully illustrated colorable images allowing readers to engage in mindfulness through coloring.

DAY 1

Be Anxious for Nothing

Don't worry about anything; instead, pray
about everything. Tell God what you need,
and thank him for all he has done.

—PHILIPPIANS 4:6 (NLT)

Do you worry? I do. I worry about many things, probably more than I should. My mother gave me my first "big kid" Bible when I was ten or eleven. On the front page, she wrote the scripture "Phil. 4:4–6." Maybe she knew I would need it.

I am highly organized, efficient, and sometimes anxious. Because I operate from a place of being organized and managing logistics easily, I often worry about what will happen, what has occurred, and what if. In the book of Philippians, Paul tells us to rejoice in the Lord and worry about nothing but instead pray about everything.

What does it mean to pray about everything? I take it to mean praying about everything literally. I worry about things like my kids, work, my ability to complete a task, money, or things that may never happen. When we look at praying about everything, it's taking everything that troubles us to God. For example, I served as a chief of staff in a governmental organization where things moved quickly. I was responsible for coordinating daily tasks and working with other executives. This job caused me a lot of anxiety. I had tight deadlines and made decisions quickly, and there was little margin for mistakes.

One day, I needed to send a report to my boss. I had been waiting for some information from a colleague to complete the report. I had asked for it sometime before but still had not received it. I became very nervous when my boss asked for the report by noon that morning. I thought of emailing my colleague again to request the information. I also thought about sending the report as is and sharing that I'd never received the additional information from my colleague. Neither option sat well with me. My colleague had a lot of work to manage and probably did not get to it.

Instead, I decided to pray about it. I asked God to help me. I told Him this report was due, and I needed this information to get it to my boss on time. After praying, I opened my inbox to start emailing my colleague; then I heard a whisper, "Wait." I stopped typing and waited. About a minute later, my colleague emailed the information I had been waiting for. I finished the report and submitted it to my boss on time.

To pray about everything means just that. Be confident that whatever issue you face, big or small, you can take it to God. He cares about what we care about. So often, God seems so far away from us. Perhaps this is because we cannot see Him. But through praying consistently, reading the Bible, dissecting what we have read, and praising God, we will feel His presence more and more around us.

When the scripture speaks about "thanksgiving," it means coming to God with thankfulness. Remind yourself of how good God has been. Focus on the situations God has already brought you through, and believe He will carry you through again.

Reflection: Reflect on a time when you were really worried about something. How did you see God move in that situation?

_____

_____

_____

_____

_____

_____

_____

_____

_____

_____

_____

_____

_____

_____

_____

Day 1 in Prayer
Use this section to write down a prayer for today.

_____

_____

_____

_____

_____

_____

_____

_____

_____

_____

_____

_____

_____

_____

_____

_____

WAIT ON THE LORD

Be joyful in hope, patient in affliction, faithful in prayer.

—ROMANS 12:12 (NIV)

There is something that happens in the "wait." Sometimes, we pray for situations that God answers quickly. It can be that day or even that very hour. But some things in life take months and even years to be answered. Situations like sickness, job loss, financial troubles, problems with our children, or a sick parent require patience. It is easy to think, *Does God hear me?*

Waiting can be very discouraging. I remember praying for my family as a teenager. We were experiencing some challenges. My mother suddenly became ill in her late forties. The doctors could not diagnose her, but she was experiencing swelling in her joints, preventing her from walking. Several months into her illness, she was diagnosed with a severe case of rheumatoid arthritis. Rheumatoid arthritis is "an autoimmune disease where the immune system attacks the healthy cells in the body, causing inflammation (painful swelling) in the affected parts of the body" (CDC 2022).

My mother managed our household while working full-time and serving as the chief operations officer for my father's business. When my mother became ill, she and my father switched roles. He now had to manage the household, care for me and my mom, and run his business. Two years after that, my father's mother died. The following year, my father's company nearly closed.

Our trials were back-to-back during that season. I asked God to help my family get back on track. I prayed that prayer for years.

Eventually, my father's business recovered. Over time, my mother regained mobility. She was able to walk and manage her pain. As a family, we spent time together, communicated, and enjoyed one another's company. I remember thinking, *Thank You, God, for hearing my prayers all these years.*

Waiting is not about inaction but about patience. Waiting is believing, by faith, that God will answer you no matter how long the answer takes. Sometimes, the silence is an opportunity for us to seek God and better understand what we need to learn from that season. Wait until you get clear direction on what to do. How often do we seek God first? We take a job opportunity, engage in a discussion we were unprepared for, move to a new city, and so on. We think we know what we need. But the Bible is clear: God wants to guide us. Will you wait for Him?

Reflection: What prevents you from waiting on God?

_____

_____

_____

_____

_____

_____

_____

_____

_____

_____

_____

_____

_____

_____

Day 2 in Prayer
Use this section to write down a prayer for today.

_____

_____

_____

_____

_____

_____

_____

_____

_____

_____

_____

_____

_____

_____

_____

_____

_____

Joy Comes in the Morning

*Those who sow in tears shall
reap with shouts of joy!*

—PSALM 126:5 (ESV)

*Come quickly, Lord, and answer me, for my
depression deepens. Don't turn away from
me, or I will die. Let me hear of your unfailing
love each morning, for I am trusting you. Show
me where to walk, for I give myself to you.*

—PSALM 143:7–8 (NLT)

*In my distress I prayed to the Lord, and
the Lord answered me and set me free.*

—PSALM 118:5 (NLT)

In Psalm 30:5, David tells us that weeping may endure for a night, but joy comes in the morning. How long have you been waiting for morning to come? I assure you that even though you cannot see it right now, your morning is coming. It may seem dark right now, but the breakthrough is coming. Even if you feel like the pressure hasn't let up, you don't have any answers, or you don't know what to do, joy will come. That's a promise.

I battled depression in my early twenties. By all accounts, I should have been "happy." I was completing my master's degree in social work. I had a cute little studio apartment with a pool. I had great friends, partied most weekends, and worked part-time on campus. I had no cares at all.

Yet when I sat in that apartment, it felt dark and like the walls were closing in on me. I cried myself to sleep many nights. I wanted to be happy. I wanted to enjoy my life, but I had been through so much by then that it was hard to see the forest from the trees. Emotionally, I was struggling.

One thing I did consistently was pray. I prayed for God to save me. I asked Him to remove my negative thoughts. I prayed and prayed, believing He heard me when I did not know how to escape the darkness. This was a very challenging season. I was learning about the importance of mental health and self-care in school, but I was so far from any of it. Eventually, I gathered enough courage to find a therapist and began climbing out of the hole.

Today, I have resolved the unsettled trauma from being adopted and have overcome low self-esteem. I now believe that I am worthy of receiving God's love. I have been in therapy for nearly twenty years, on and off. And I am just believing in who God says I am.

Wherever you find yourself today, that is perfectly OK. Do not judge yourself, but be honest about where you are. The morning will come. Continue to push through the darkness. The sun will shine again.

Reflection: Close your eyes. Imagine what your life will be like when the sun finally comes up. Write down what you saw.

_____

_____

_____

_____

_____

_____

_____

_____

_____

_____

_____

_____

_____

Day 3 in Prayer
Use this section to write down a prayer for today.

_____

_____

_____

_____

_____

_____

_____

_____

_____

_____

_____

_____

_____

_____

_____

_____

_____

RESOLUTION

And "don't sin by letting anger control you."
Don't let the sun go down while you are still
angry, for anger gives a foothold to the devil.

—EPHESIANS 4:26–27 (NLT)

Do all that you can to live in peace with everyone.

—ROMANS 12:18 (NLT)

In recent years, I have focused on better understanding how to address conflict. I work to resolve disagreements quickly and gracefully. But some situations take time to settle. How do you approach conflict? Do you face it head-on, ready to discuss your side of the situation, while waiting eagerly to hear the other person's perspective? Do you come prepared to fight? Do you run, hoping that if enough time passes, the other person will forget about it somehow?

No matter how you approach conflict, the Bible says we must forgive those who trespass against us. The word is *trespass* in the King James Version; but you may say the person who "crossed you," "dissed you," "tricked you," "used you," "manipulated you," "abused you," or "took advantage of you." Whichever category fits your situation, how do you get to a place of resolution?

Sometimes, a resolution is not possible. I think about instances where an individual has passed away or moved to a new state, and you do not have an address or phone number for them. In those cases, you may be unable to speak with the person to get a resolution. But we can take the issue to God.

Harboring anger, frustration, bitterness, and resentment can manifest in our bodies as we continue to carry the transgression or offense. Jesus says in 1 Peter 5:7 (CSB), "Cast your cares on me." Casting your cares on Jesus means telling Him what you are worried about or what scares you and sharing the things you cannot tell anyone else. Tell Him everything. We can trust God to handle it. He wants to be at the center of our lives to show us how to love others even when we do not feel like it.

Reflection: Who do you need to forgive? As you reflect, consider if you need to forgive yourself. If so, start there.

_____

_____

_____

_____

_____

_____

_____

_____

_____

_____

_____

_____

_____

Day 4 in Prayer
Use this section to write down a prayer for today.

_____

_____

_____

_____

_____

_____

_____

_____

_____

_____

_____

_____

_____

_____

_____

_____

_____

Pray When You Don't Feel Like It

*Therefore I tell you, whatever you ask
for in prayer, believe that you have
received it, and it will be yours.*

—MARK 11:24 (NIV)

*Call to me and I will answer you and tell you
great and unsearchable things you do not know.*

—JEREMIAH 33:3 (NIV)

Yep. You read the title correctly. There is such a thing as not feeling like praying. I am not talking about laziness. I'm talking about being so discouraged, disappointed, anxious, or depressed that you cannot muster up the strength to get past *God*.

I remember when my father died. I was twenty-nine years old. We had been preparing to purchase my first home. I say *we* because this was a family event. I recall my parents being excited and proud of me. My father was a mechanical engineer. He could fix anything. The plan for the home search included him estimating the costs of repairs or enhancements that might be needed. I had been shopping in the housing market for three months. Then, one day, my dad had a heart attack and died—just like that. One day, we were house shopping; the next day, he was gone.

My father's death was so sudden. When he died, I felt like I couldn't breathe. It seemed like I was gasping for air, and I could not sleep. Going to church felt confusing in the early days, weeks, and months after his death. I was sad. I was angry. I was confused. I wanted more time. But it was over. I didn't know how to pray. I had no idea what to say to God. I was lost.

It would be years later before I would find some semblance of peace.

There are seasons when life will bring us to our knees. Death. Calamity. Divorce. Illness. Betrayal. These devastations, and many others, can leave us helpless. But God knows what we need, what we're thinking, and how we're feeling. If all you can muster up is "God, help me," the scripture tells us the Holy Spirit intercedes for us with groanings we cannot understand (Romans 8:26 NLT). God will hear you. He always hears you. Trust that He will respond no matter how complex your situation is, and accept that the answer may not be exactly what you wanted.

Even if you feel like you can't pray or don't know what to pray for, the Lord wants to hear from you and assures us that the Holy Spirit will intercede on our behalf if we are at a loss for words. Just call on Him, and He'll do the rest.

Reflection: What do you need to release to God?

_____

_____

_____

_____

_____

_____

_____

_____

_____

_____

_____

_____

_____

_____

Day 5 in Prayer
Use this section to write down a prayer for today.

_____

_____

_____

_____

_____

_____

_____

_____

_____

_____

_____

_____

_____

_____

_____

_____

_____

DAY
6

DECISIONS, DECISIONS, DECISIONS

"For I know the plans I have for you," declares the Lord, "plans to prosper you and not to harm you, plans to give you hope and a future."

—JEREMIAH 29:11 (NIV)

I shared on Day 1 that I get anxious at times. During the pandemic, I wanted to buy a bigger house to have a fourth bedroom for our one-year-old daughter and guests. I searched for homes for over a year. I narrowed my search down to one specific city. One day, my husband told me God told him to pray over every city we wanted to live in. I told you I narrowed it down to one, but we had five cities on our list. We wanted to be obedient, even though I wondered what this would look like.

One Friday afternoon, my husband and I drove to all five cities and prayed as we drove through them. A few weeks later, I was combing my hair and heard a soft voice say, "Go to Fontana." Let me pause here. Fontana was not on the list. Not at all. We knew nothing about this place. OK, I'll continue.

I responded to the soft voice, saying, "Fontana? I thought we were moving to Eastvale [our top choice]." But I heard nothing back. I moved through my initial confusion and started looking for homes in Fontana. Within a month, we would find a new housing development in North Fontana that we loved! We have lived in this community for over two years.

I can't tell you how many decisions I made without consulting God and later regretted. We all experience this. The important thing is not to be so hard on ourselves but to seek God and try again. We don't know much, but God wants to show us His plans for our lives.

Reflection: When do you have a hard time trusting God (for example, with your children, your finances, your marriage, or your identity)?

_____

_____

_____

_____

_____

_____

_____

_____

_____

_____

_____

_____

_____

_____

Day 6 in Prayer
Use this section to write down a prayer for today.

_____

_____

_____

_____

_____

_____

_____

_____

_____

_____

_____

_____

_____

_____

_____

_____

GOD SEES YOU

*Then she called the name of the Lord who spoke
to her, You-Are-the-God-Who-Sees; for she said,
"Have I also here seen Him who sees me?"*

—GENESIS 16:13 (NKJV)

What would you say if I told you that God sees you? Do you believe He sees you? God is omnipresent, meaning He is present everywhere at once. That may feel scary if you are hearing this truth for the first time. But the beauty in this is that God is always with us. When I am in trouble, He's there. He's there when I am stuck on the freeway trying to get home safely. When I am out in the streets doing what I know I do not need to do, He is there too. Wherever we are, He is there with us. I hope it comforts you to know that no matter where you find yourself, good or bad, God will be there with you.

During my graduate studies, I had the opportunity to travel to the Philippines to study social work. After spending ten days overseas, I flew back on a twelve–plus–hour flight, anxious to get to the beauty salon, so much so that I called my beautician while deboarding at the airport. I scheduled an appointment for the next morning.

The next day, I drove to the salon. I was sitting at a solid green light, waiting to make a left turn. I looked, and the way was clear. There were no oncoming cars. As I began turning the wheel, I heard, "Stop." It is important to note that this was the first time I remember actually hearing God. After I heard this, I said, "But no cars are coming."

Completing this thought, I turned my car left. As I entered the intersection, I saw a pickup truck coming right at me—fast. My car was t-boned—hit on the middle of the passenger side doors. My car spun out and landed on the street corner.

Here is what happened. When I began to make the left turn, unbeknownst to me, there was a pickup truck that was parked at the curb. He then pulled out from the curb, taking the green light. As I looked for the second time, I saw the truck entering the intersection, crashing into me. I was taken away from the accident in an ambulance. I had a sprained neck and spine, and I dislocated my left shoulder. My car was totaled. Recovery from this major accident took months. I could not sit up or walk for long periods. I could barely sleep because of the pain. How I wish I had listened.

I could have avoided that accident. But how often do we do this? We hear something that makes no sense to us, shrug it off, and move forward. I did not understand why God told me to stop, so without understanding, I made a conscious decision to disregard what I heard. God sees us. The real question is, are we listening to Him?

Reflection: What distracts you from hearing God? In what ways does the Lord speak to you?

_____

_____

_____

_____

_____

_____

_____

_____

_____

_____

_____

_____

_____

_____

Day 7 in Prayer

Use this section to write down a prayer for today.

_____

_____

_____

_____

_____

_____

_____

_____

_____

_____

_____

_____

_____

_____

_____

_____

DAY

8

WHY IS THIS
HAPPENING TO ME?

Be on your guard; stand firm in the faith; be courageous; be strong. Do everything in love.

—1 CORINTHIANS 16:13-14 (NIV)

Let perseverance finish its work so that you may be mature and complete, not lacking anything.

—JAMES 1:4 (NIV)

Blessed is the one who perseveres under trial because, having stood the test, that person will receive the crown of life that the Lord has promised to those who love him.

—JAMES 1:12 (NIV)

I asked a colleague, "Why is this happening to me?" She responded, "Be careful asking questions like that." Sometimes, life feels that way. Why me? What did I do? We often seek understanding when we face challenges and mishaps. We pray, go to church, seek advice, overanalyze, or do anything to get answers.

But what if this is not happening to you? What if God allows the difficulty, the wilderness, to take you to the next level of your life? So often, with the characters of the Bible, we see regular, ordinary men and women called to accomplish extraordinary things with the power of God moving and orchestrating exchanges and events.

Instead of taking a negative perspective on your wilderness, ask God what He wants to teach you there. Ask Him to give you the strength, peace, and patience to endure until He says this season is over. Just because things are not going well in your life does not necessarily mean that you have done something wrong. God is perhaps using this season to strengthen your faith and endurance so you can become who you need to be in the next chapter of your life.

What about you? Can God trust you with difficulty? Do you become unrecognizable when you are in despair? James tells us to do everything in love. That can be extremely arduous when you feel like you are under attack for no good reason. In these difficult moments, I implore you to ask God to fortify your mind and heart so you can stand firm during trials and tribulations.

Reflection: Where do you need God to strengthen you?

_____

_____

_____

_____

_____

_____

_____

_____

_____

_____

_____

_____

_____

_____

Day 8 in Prayer
Use this section to write down a prayer for today.

_____

_____

_____

_____

_____

_____

_____

_____

_____

_____

_____

_____

_____

_____

_____

Put Aside Every Weight

Therefore, since we are surrounded by such a huge crowd of witnesses to the life of faith, let us strip off every weight that slows us down, especially the sin that so easily trips us up. And let us run with endurance the race God has set before us.

—HEBREWS 12:1 (NLT)

Since you have heard about Jesus and have learned the truth that comes from him, throw off your old sinful nature and your former way of life, which is corrupted by lust and deception. Instead, let the Spirit renew your thoughts and attitudes. Put on your new nature, created to be like God—truly righteous and holy.

—EPHESIANS 4:21-24 (NLT)

When we initially accept Jesus Christ as our Savior, we are free from sin and receive salvation through our belief that Jesus is the Son of God who lived, died, was resurrected, and now sits at the right hand of God. Living out our salvation requires that we fight our sinful nature. The natural part of us that wants to live our lives how we like to, regardless of whether it is aligned with God's principles, is referred to as our flesh. Though we are renewed in Christ, we still struggle with our flesh. In the New Testament, the Bible tells us to live as Jesus Christ lived. He is our example.

To lay aside every weight is to talk about those hang-ups, attitudes, thought patterns, and behaviors that keep us from living a life that pleases God. One of my hang-ups is perfection. I know perfection is impossible to achieve. Even with this understanding, I find myself striving for a standard that does not exist. I have little grace for myself when I do not achieve what I set out to do. Focusing on being perfect expounds on a false belief that I am not good enough the way I am. But somehow, if I am perfect, people will accept or love me. This was an unconscious belief I held for many years. That need for perfection prevented me from truly being myself and engaging in authentic relationships with others.

God cannot bless who you pretend to be. This thought pattern was rooted in rejection and worthlessness. I have gotten much better over the years. I still struggle at times, but I put the weight aside daily.

Reflection: What weight are you carrying? What gets in the way of fully walking into the life God calls you to? Whatever it is, God will help you if you give it to Him.

_____

_____

_____

_____

_____

_____

_____

_____

_____

_____

_____

_____

_____

Day 9 in Prayer
Use this section to write down a prayer for today.

_____

_____

_____

_____

_____

_____

_____

_____

_____

_____

_____

_____

_____

_____

_____

_____

_____

DAY

10

Make Peace with Your Story

Then you will experience God's peace,
which exceeds anything we can understand.
His peace will guard your hearts and
minds as you live in Christ Jesus.

—PHILIPPIANS 4:7 (NLT)

Throughout my life, I have reflected on many experiences, asking God why I had to go through certain situations. I can tell you that I am still waiting for answers. I am reassured by how God filled in the gaps throughout my life.

My biological mother loved her children but was seriously addicted to drugs. Child welfare had to intervene. I was blessed to be adopted by my maternal aunt and uncle. God gave me capable parents who were wise, loved God, and sacrificed much of themselves. And still, I struggled with issues of abandonment and attachment.

I did not like sharing my story. I was embarrassed to tell people I was adopted. I worried they would pity me. It is challenging to grow up feeling unwanted. In adolescence, I wrestled with being accepted and feeling worthy of love, though I had two loving parents.

Today, after much prayer, formal education, and tons of therapy, I have a better understanding of my trauma. I accept that some things will not be answered during my lifetime. With it all, I have lived an extraordinary life thus far. The scripture is true: my latter days have been better than my former days.

What part of your story are you struggling with? Does it involve mental health or substance abuse? Were you the product of sexual violence? Were your parents divorced? Did you grow up in foster care? Whatever your story, the sooner you accept the fact that you are still here despite the pain you experienced, the sooner you will find peace. Jesus will comfort you, counsel you, and fight your battles. If forgiveness is a part of the story you need to address, read Day 16 to begin working through that weight.

Minister Thomas A. Whitfield sang a song called "Hallelujah Anyhow." The entire song only has two words: *hallelujah* and *anyhow*. But if you listen, I promise it will bring you to tears.

What does it mean to praise God anyhow? It suggests that no matter what the circumstances are, praise God. Sing a song of worship or dance. Thank God simply for who He is, even when you are disappointed. Some experiences in our lives have nothing to do with God. Some things we experience are the result of others' mistakes or choices.

My biological mother's drug addiction adversely affected our entire family. I cannot blame God for that. Substance use disorder is very complex. She had a severe condition that she could not control. Recognizing this fact has given me solace and stopped me from continuing to hold on to the fact that she was absent from my life.

I had to make peace with my story. I had to accept who I am and how I got here. I look at God's grace in providing me with parents who loved me. That is God.

Find peace through seeking God. He will give you solitude and fill in the gaps in your life.

Reflection: What parts of your story do you need to make peace with? Reflect on who you are today.

_____

_____

_____

_____

_____

_____

_____

_____

_____

_____

_____

_____

_____

_____

_____

Day 10 in Prayer
Use this section to write down a prayer for today.

_____

_____

_____

_____

_____

_____

_____

_____

_____

_____

_____

_____

_____

_____

_____

_____

Don't Look Back

*But Lot's wife looked back as she was following
behind him, and she turned into a pillar of salt.*

—GENESIS 19:26 (NLT)

You may not know the story of Lot's wife, but her story is a tale of longing for what was instead of being obedient and trusting where God was taking her.

Lot (Abraham's nephew) and his family lived in the city of Sodom. Gomorrah was a neighboring city. Sodom and Gomorrah were full of wickedness and sin, so much so that the Lord decided to destroy them. God sent two of His angels to destroy the cities. But God was merciful; the angels told Lot to escape with his family before the destruction (Genesis 19:12–16). He was instructed to run for his life and not look back or stop anywhere in the valley. The Lord rained down fire and sulfur from the sky on Sodom and Gomorrah, destroying it and the neighboring villages and cities. As Lot and his family ran to safety, his wife looked back, yearning for what she lost; she immediately turned into a pillar of salt. Lot's wife was unable to escape because of her disobedience.

What has God called you out of that you keep returning to? God will provide a means of escape, but we must take it. We cannot keep focusing on the person who left us or that incident that hurt us and still expect to be healed in a new chapter of our lives. Holding on to the past prevents us from walking into the future God has prepared for us.

God wants to release you from that bondage, no matter how hard the rejection was, how painful the betrayal was, or how badly you might have messed up. He whom the Son sets free is free indeed (John 8:36 NIV). We can be free if we choose to accept it. Our healing must be intentional. It will require work from us. A part of that work is releasing our past. You have a choice to make. Will you go where God is calling you? Don't look back.

Reflection: How can you move forward in this season of your life?

_____

_____

_____

_____

_____

_____

_____

_____

_____

_____

_____

_____

_____

Day 11 in Prayer
Use this section to write down a prayer for today.

_____

_____

_____

_____

_____

_____

_____

_____

_____

_____

_____

_____

_____

_____

_____

_____

PRAY UNTIL SOMETHING HAPPENS (PUSH)

For we [not relying on the Law but] through the [strength and power of the Holy] Spirit, by faith, are waiting [confidently] for the hope of righteousness [the completion of our salvation].

—GALATIANS 5:5 (AMP)

In the beginning was the Word, and the Word was with God, and the Word was God. He was with God in the beginning. Through him all things were made; without him nothing was made that has been made. In him was life, and that life was the light of all mankind. The light shines in the darkness, and the darkness has not overcome it.

—JOHN 1:1-5 (NIV)

About three years ago, God used several people to tell me that I would have a son. When this occurred, I had just given birth to my second daughter. The idea of having a third child was overwhelming. I recall one afternoon when I was nursing my daughter, and I heard God whisper, "You will find your way." That stuck with me.

In challenging times, when I feel inadequate as a mom, I say to myself, *I will find my way.* When I am having a hard day, I say this repeatedly. When I forget to pack the kids' lunches for school, or I am late to the pediatric appointment because I got off work late, I remember God's Word, and I reassure myself that this mothering journey will all come together eventually. What has God promised you?

Remember what God has said about your life. It will help you in the difficult days. We may not know the time or the day, but if God said it, it will surely come to pass. Trust Him.

Reflection: How can you use the Word of God to reassure yourself during challenging times?

_____

_____

_____

_____

_____

_____

_____

_____

_____

_____

_____

_____

_____

_____

Day 12 in Prayer
Use this section to write down a prayer for today.

_____

_____

_____

_____

_____

_____

_____

_____

_____

_____

_____

_____

_____

_____

LET HIM USE YOU

*Rejoice in the Lord always. I will say it
again: Rejoice! Let your gentleness be
evident to all. The Lord is near.*

—PHILIPPIANS 4:4–5 (NIV)

*Take delight in the Lord, and he will
give you the desires of your heart.*

—PSALM 37:4 (NIV)

"What's in your hand?" That's the question God asked Moses when He spoke to him about bringing the people of Israel out of bondage in Egypt (Exodus 3:10 and 4:2). Moses questioned his calling from God, thinking what he had was not good enough. Moses had a stamper in his speech. His stutter made him insecure, but God used what Moses had to fulfill His promise to His people, the children of Israel. When Moses protested against God's calling of him, God suggested he use his brother Aaron to speak to the people of Israel (Exodus 4:14). God used Moses to carry out His will.

What's in your hand? What does God want to use that you're ashamed of or embarrassed by? I believe that God desires to use my story to help others face and heal from their trauma. I have to admit that it is difficult for me to rest with the idea that God can use me. Little old me? Yes, me. And God can use your story too. God created us in His likeness. We are fearfully and wonderfully made. What He has given us is more than enough to fulfill our purpose. You are not here by accident or happenstance. Don't believe that lie no matter who told it to you.

We need to be willing to answer God's call. He can and will use anything He wants to accomplish His plan for our lives and the lives of others. Will you let Him use you?

Reflection: What has God asked you to do that you have not acted on?

_____

_____

_____

_____

_____

_____

_____

_____

_____

_____

_____

_____

_____

_____

Day 13 in Prayer
Use this section to write down a prayer for today.

_____

_____

_____

_____

_____

_____

_____

_____

_____

_____

_____

_____

_____

_____

_____

OBEDIENCE IS BETTER
THAN SACRIFICE

*But Samuel replied, "What is more pleasing to
the Lord: your burnt offerings and sacrifices or
your obedience to his voice? Listen! Obedience
is better than sacrifice, and submission is
better than offering the fat of rams."*

—1 SAMUEL 15:22 (NLT)

What is the first thing that comes to mind when you think of obedience? Are you eager for the opportunity to obey, or do you resist? I am very strong-willed, so listening to others can be challenging at times. During the COVID-19 pandemic, there wasn't much to do. We sheltered in place in our home. Schools were closed, and my job moved entirely online.

After a couple of weeks, I became more comfortable being at home all day. I know the pandemic was not a pleasant time for every household. I liked being able to slow things down. Before 2020, I was busy. I worked full-time as a supervisor, commuting to and from work three to five hours per day. I managed a household; cared for my two children, one of whom was a newborn at the time; volunteered for various committees at my church; and tried spending much-needed time with my husband whenever I could. It was hard to designate time to pray, though I went to church twice a week, volunteered in the young adult ministry, and participated in the new mommies' class. Our lives were hectic.

I prayed often, but I needed a prayer routine. Being at home, I watched a lot of movies. One day, I watched a film called *War Room*, where this woman struggling in her marriage met an older woman who told her to fight her battles by praying in her closet. I was very inspired after watching it. I cleaned out my closet to make room where I could sit and began praying each morning.

What interested me about the film was the idea that I could hear more clearly from God if I had a designated place to pray. Well, it was true! When I started praying in my closet in the mornings and evenings, I clearly heard God. There were countless moments when I had clear directions from Him.

I recall one evening, after nursing my five-month-old daughter, she kept crying. She screamed and hollered for what felt like an hour. I was already sleep-deprived and exhausted. I remember asking God to help me. "Why is this happening? What am I doing wrong?" As I asked a barrage of questions, I heard, "This is not about you." *This is not about me?* I thought. This is happening to *me*.

Then, I realized that if this is not about me, it must be regarding my daughter. I immediately tried to nurse her again. As I attempted to nurse, she kept screaming at my breast. I tried massaging the milk ducts so the milk would release. The milk was not coming out.

That was it! No wonder she was screaming her head off; she was hungry! Fortunately, I had some formula bottles in the kitchen. I grabbed one and fed her immediately. She ate the entire bottle and then stopped crying. Spending designated time in prayer allowed me to be attuned to God's voice. Would you recognize God's voice if you heard it?

Make time to get closer to God through prayer. Even if it's five minutes per day, that's a start. God will honor your efforts. He wants to be in a relationship with us. If we seek Him, He will draw closer to us.

Reflection: How can you spend more time in prayer?

_____

_____

_____

_____

_____

_____

_____

_____

_____

_____

_____

_____

_____

_____

Day 14 in Prayer

Use this section to write down a prayer for today.

_____

_____

_____

_____

_____

_____

_____

_____

_____

_____

_____

_____

_____

_____

_____

_____

Take Every Thought Captive

We destroy every proud obstacle that keeps people from knowing God. We capture their rebellious thoughts and teach them to obey Christ.

—2 CORINTHIANS 10:5 (NLT)

For as he thinks in his heart, so is he.

—PROVERBS 23:7 (NKJV)

Finally, believers, whatever is true, whatever is honorable and worthy of respect, whatever is right and confirmed by God's Word, whatever is pure and wholesome, whatever is lovely and brings peace, whatever is admirable and of good repute; if there is any excellence, if there is anything worthy of praise, think continually on these things [center your mind on them, and implant them in your heart].

—PHILIPPIANS 4:8 (AMP)

The Bible provides us with countless scriptures on how we should think. In the book of 2 Corinthians, we are reminded that we have the authority to take control of our thoughts and make them obedient to Christ. When I think about the power of our thoughts, I like the application of Joshua 1:8 NIV, which says, "Keep this Book of the Law always on your lips; meditate on it day and night, so that you may be careful to do everything written in it." Through meditation on the Word of God, we can replace negative thinking with scriptures while focusing on those things that are true and worthy of praise.

From a clinical perspective, the evidence-based intervention called cognitive behavioral therapy (CBT) focuses on "helping them [individuals] to understand their current ways of thinking and behaving and equipping them with the tools to change their maladaptive cognitive and behavioral patterns" (Fenn and Byrne 2013). Our thoughts and behaviors are connected. CBT believes that by focusing on changing negative or unhealthy thought patterns and replacing them with more accurate thinking, individuals can improve their well-being. Through skilled facilitation with a therapist, CBT techniques are applied to address various mental health conditions, including anxiety, depression, panic attacks, posttraumatic stress disorder, and others.

Physicist and author Leonard Mlodinow, in his book *Emotional: How Feelings Shape Our Thinking* (2022), highlights some new science that found "emotions affect thinking: our emotional state influences our mental calculations as much as the objective data or circumstances we are pondering." Therefore, our emotional health is connected to our thought life. The current saying, "Get out of your feelings" suggests that something is wrong with acknowledging our emotions. But what if understanding our feelings can help us heal?

Whether you find yourself aligned with current emotion science or are a fan of CBT, addressing your overall emotional health can improve how you think about yourself and the world around you.

Reflection: When was the last time you felt a powerful emotion? What was that feeling? Reflect on the thoughts and behaviors that followed those feelings. Look for connections.

_____

_____

_____

_____

_____

_____

_____

_____

_____

_____

_____

_____

_____

_____

Day 15 in Prayer

Use this section to write down a prayer for today.

_____

_____

_____

_____

_____

_____

_____

_____

_____

_____

_____

_____

_____

_____

_____

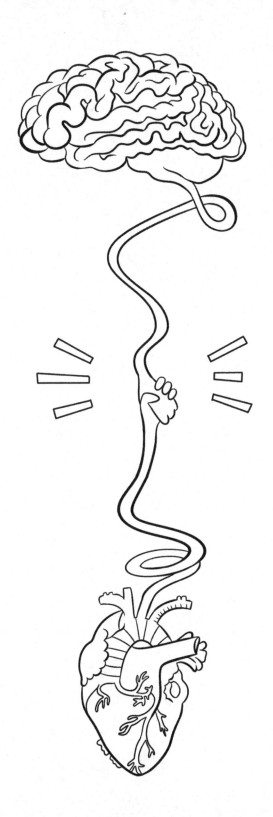

FORGIVE YOURSELF

*Therefore, there is now no condemnation
for those who are in Christ Jesus.*

—ROMANS 8:1(NIV)

How often do we pick up things that God has already forgiven? When we think about being free spiritually, we must come to peace with our mistakes. Jesus died for our sins. This does not mean we will never sin again once we receive salvation, but it means we should sin less because we know how to live a life that is pleasing to God. Jesus's death and resurrection means we are forgiven. But if we are honest, we may still carry guilt, shame, or embarrassment.

The enemy wants to keep us bound by reminding us of our mistakes. Be not deceived. You are forgiven. You can begin to forgive yourself by being honest about what happened. Take accountability for your role in the situation and release the aspects that were out of your control.

If you need to apologize to someone, then do so. If you need help doing that, write the person a letter. You do not need to send it. Write down everything that you want to say. Then, shred the letter and throw it away. The key is to release it and not repeat the behavior! Remind yourself of Romans 8:1. Say it to yourself aloud. Write it out and post it on the bathroom mirror, car dashboard, refrigerator, or garage. Just be sure the truth is visible to remind you of your freedom.

My hope is that you embrace the freedom from sin that Jesus provides and forgive yourself. You are a new creation in Christ.

Reflection: What mistakes do you need to forgive yourself for?

_____

_____

_____

_____

_____

_____

_____

_____

_____

_____

_____

_____

_____

Day 16 in Prayer
Use this section to write down a prayer for today.

_____

_____

_____

_____

_____

_____

_____

_____

_____

_____

_____

_____

_____

_____

_____

DAY

17

WAIT IN THE WAIT

*Yet I am confident I will see the Lord's goodness
while I am here in the land of the living.
Wait patiently for the Lord. Be brave and
courageous. Yes, wait patiently for the Lord.*

PSALM 27:13–14 (NLT)

There is a popular contemporary Christian gospel song called "Wait on You" by Elevation Worship and Maverick City. It is so beautifully sung, with live instruments and a mass choir ushering in the Holy Spirit through praise and worship. But when the song goes off and the choir stops singing, we are left doing just that: waiting.

Waiting is one of the most complex parts of the faith journey. *Merriam-Webster* defines *wait* as the ability "to stay in place in expectation of." Expectation? How often do we sit waiting and thinking, *Is God going to answer my prayer? Did He hear me? What am I supposed to do now? When is God going to answer?* Waiting with expectation means anticipating He will answer. Expectations have confidence.

Often, we focus on what is not happening instead of waiting on God with anticipation that He is answering our prayers. How do we stay in the wait? The wait is the long period between when you ask God to do something and when you see an answer. The wait is an opportunity for us to draw closer to God. Spending more time with God through praying, meditating, journaling, and reading our Bible will help us attain peace while waiting for Him. It builds our confidence and trust in Him.

It is important to remember that God's ways are not ours, and His thoughts are not our thoughts (Isaiah 55:8). Our prayers may not be answered as we imagine. But we continue to wait on Him, knowing He will complete the good work He started in us.

Waiting requires trust. Do you trust God with everything you have? Reflect on that. You may find that you do not trust Him with everything, which often leads to anxiety over situations we cannot control. But I urge you to wait on Him. He will never fail you. His love is everlasting. He knows what we need before we need it, so wait confidently.

Reflection: How can you wait differently?

_____

_____

_____

_____

_____

_____

_____

_____

_____

_____

_____

_____

_____

_____

Day 17 in Prayer

Use this section to write down a prayer for today.

WAIT on the LORD

PULLING DOWN OF STRONGHOLDS: ANGER

For if you forgive other people when they sin against you, your heavenly Father will also forgive you.

—MATTHEW 6:14 (NIV)

Control your temper, for anger labels you a fool.

—ECCLESIASTES 7:9 (NLT)

Often, anger results from someone or something that offended us, intentionally or unintentionally. Forgiveness is about us, not the person who offended us. Forgiveness—true forgiveness—releases a weight from the heart, bringing a sense of resolve and peace, thereby releasing pent-up anger, frustration, disappointment, depression, bitterness, self-loathing, rejection, isolation, sadness, or loneliness that weighs the heart down.

Anger is a natural defense mechanism. The real work begins when we seek to understand the underlying need behind our anger. Do you feel unsafe, embarrassed, ignored, misunderstood, or disrespected? A myriad of emotions can result in the outward expression of anger. It is important for us to seek understanding behind our feelings. This will help us have better self-control.

Forgiveness is hard. Pain can be so deep we feel like we cannot possibly forgive others. But through prayer, God can help us see the situation differently. We can gain empathy for others, helping us move toward forgiveness and healing. We gain freedom through forgiving others.

Reflection: Reflect on the last time you were angry. What was the underlying emotion you were feeling? What would you do differently if you could do it all over again?

_____

_____

_____

_____

_____

_____

_____

_____

_____

_____

_____

_____

_____

_____

Day 18 in Prayer

Use this section to write down a prayer for today.

_____

_____

_____

_____

_____

_____

_____

_____

_____

_____

_____

_____

_____

_____

CONTROL AIN'T FAITH

*We can make our own plans, but the
Lord gives the right answer.*

—PROVERBS 16:1(NLT)

*I took my troubles to the Lord; I cried out
to him, and he answered my prayer.*

PSALM 120:1 (NLT)

No one wants to admit to being controlling. The funny thing is, no one has absolute control over anything. Control creates a false sense of security. And yet, some people spend considerable time trying to control as much as possible. I'll use myself as an example.

I can be very controlling. It manifests in many ways, from planning every aspect of my day to fixating on how I will accomplish various things in my life. This carries over into my parenting. I think about different scenarios that might come up for the kids as I plan for them. It is mentally exhausting. And, frankly, impossible. Only God knows everything. So why do we keep trying to be God? That is what we attempt to do.

Being in control has nothing to do with God. It is more of a reflection of our lack of faith in His ability to provide for us. Are you offended by that? Good. I want you to be offended so you will begin to relinquish control to the only one who knows everything, is everywhere at once, and provides every good thing to us: God. I may sound preachy, but that is more for my sake than yours. I need help in this area too. Trust that God will give you divine instruction when you need it. Our job is to trust Him and do the work.

Reflection: What scares you about not being in control?

_____

_____

_____

_____

_____

_____

_____

_____

_____

_____

_____

_____

_____

_____

_____

Day 19 in Prayer
Use this section to write down a prayer for today.

DAY

20

Faith without Works Is Dead

Then Jesus said to the centurion, "Go! Let it be done just as you believed it would." And his servant was healed at that moment.

—MATTHEW 8:13 (NIV)

What are you believing God for: healing in your body, a healthy marriage, or help for your child? How are you doing your part in it?

We bring our cares to God when we pray. But there is another element that we must do. We cannot just pray and wait to see what happens. We must do the work. I work hard, but in recent years, I have tried not to overwork myself. I focus on not overcommitting, keeping my schedule light, focusing on family time, and not doing too much.

Around the fall of 2023, the Lord told me plainly that I was complacent. This message was confirmed later through a post by a Christian woman I follow on social media and other devotional readings. It was difficult for me to understand because I am a hard worker. This idea of complacency made me think of laziness. But the two are different. Laziness refers to being unwilling to work or idleness (Dunham 2023).

Meanwhile, complacency, as I understand it, is about settling for good enough. I feel like God was telling me that there is more I have planned for you, but you are settling. He was right. I had settled into my middle-class life, career, and community. I was content with where I thought God had called me. I was working and caring for my family. But there was more that He had for me.

I had settled for doing less for so long that when I began to pursue the various things I felt God telling me to do, I started feeling overwhelmed. While praying about this season, the Lord told me, "Don't be overwhelmed." That made me think I could pursue these things while managing my emotions. It also made me realize that feeling overwhelmed was a choice in some ways. I could choose not to feel overwhelmed.

I am currently working on leaning into the discomfort of what God is calling me to. I have changed my feelings about it, seeing this as an opportunity for God to use me uniquely. The Bible tells us that God rejoices to see the work begin (Zechariah 4:10 NLT).

Reflection: What have you been praying about that requires you to take action?

_____

_____

_____

_____

_____

_____

_____

_____

_____

_____

_____

_____

_____

_____

Day 20 in Prayer

Use this section to write down a prayer for today.

_____

_____

_____

_____

_____

_____

_____

_____

_____

_____

_____

_____

_____

_____

_____

OVERWHELMED: GIVE US THIS DAY OUR DAILY BREAD

After this manner therefore pray ye: Our Father which art in heaven, Hallowed be thy name. Thy kingdom come. Thy will be done in earth, as it is in heaven. Give us this day our daily bread. And forgive us our debts, as we forgive our debtors. And lead us not into temptation, but deliver us from evil: For thine is the kingdom, and the power, and the glory, for ever. Amen.

—MATTHEW 6:9-13 (KJV)

When I feel overwhelmed, it's hard for me to think clearly. I cannot sort through everything in my head; I can't hear clearly from God and feel distracted. Being overwhelmed can be a unique opportunity to connect with God. But the enemy wants to distract us from relying on God as our source of strength, guidance, comfort, and understanding.

What can we do? I like to do a brain dump. A brain dump is where you write down everything that overwhelms you, from simple tasks to decision-making. Then, ask God to help you in each area. Tell Him honestly how you are feeling.

For example, it's picture day at your child's school. You need more money to buy a nice outfit, and their clothing is too small. Or I have a huge presentation at work, and I do not have enough time to prepare. I have overcommitted myself and am afraid to let people down.

List everything that is concerning you to God in prayer. Be specific as to what you think you need. I say *what you think you need* because the Word of God says in Romans 8:26: "We know not what to pray for as we should, but the Holy Spirit intercedes on our behalf with groanings we cannot understand." God is waiting for us to lay these problems at His feet.

In Matthew 6:11 KJV, Jesus tells the disciples how to pray in the Lord's Prayer: "Give us this day our daily bread." This verse tells us not to worry but to ask our Heavenly Father to give us what we need today. Not tomorrow, not what we need on Tuesday because the calendar is hectic, not next week, but today. Tomorrow belongs to God. If we trust Him with everything we need, He will provide. In that trust, we will experience His peace that surpasses all understanding.

In our daily walk, it's crucial to understand how the enemy comes to destroy us. One tactic is to overwhelm us with persistent attacks, wearing us down to the point that we can't fight. We don't want to fight. We isolate ourselves. Have you heard the saying, "When it rains, it pours"? When people say that, I interpret that as they can't take another thing happening simultaneously. It's too much. But in times like this, we should pray diligently, seeking God's face constantly, not necessarily so our circumstances will change, because they may not, but so we can gain the strength, courage, and peace we need to get through the day. And then, guess what? You will do the same thing again tomorrow to press through that day. Our persistence, the Bible says, builds endurance. So, keep going!

May the God who gives endurance and encouragement give you the same attitude of mind toward each other that Christ Jesus had. May the God of hope fill you with all joy and peace as you trust in Him, so that you may overflow with hope by the power of the Holy Spirit (Romans 15:5, 15:13 NIV).

Reflection: What helps you feel less overwhelmed?

_____

_____

_____

_____

_____

_____

_____

_____

_____

_____

_____

_____

_____

Day 21 in Prayer
Use this section to write down a prayer for today.

_____

_____

_____

_____

_____

_____

_____

_____

_____

_____

_____

_____

_____

_____

STRENGTHEN YOURSELF

But this is what the Sovereign Lord says: "This invasion will never happen; it will never take place, for Syria is no stronger than its capital, Damascus, and Damascus is no stronger than its king, Rezin. As for Israel, within sixty-five years, it will be crushed and completely destroyed. Israel is no stronger than its capital, Samaria, and Samaria is no stronger than its king, Pekah son of Remaliah. Unless your faith is firm, I cannot make you stand firm."

—ISAIAH 7:7–9 (NLT)

We all get to a point when we have to believe in God for ourselves. You might have grown up with parents who "weren't very religious." But your grandmother could pray to pull down heaven. Unfortunately, your grandmother's faith can only take you so far. You have to believe for yourself. Our walk with God has nothing to do with religion; it has to do with our relationship with Him.

Let me ask you something. What is dating you like? When pursuing someone you are interested in, what does that look like? Do you call and text often? Are you looking to spend as much time together to get to know them? Or are you the withdrawn type? Do you want that person to pursue you while you act less interested, hoping they will come to you? Or do you get easily distracted and forget to call or do you miss scheduled dates? Would you date yourself?

I know the dating analogy may be challenging for you to imagine when thinking about God. But to be in a relationship with God, we must pursue Him. The more we spend time with God, the more profound and substantial our faith gets. The Bible says to ask, and it shall be given unto you; seek, and you will find; knock, and the door will be opened (Matthew 7:7). God is waiting for us to seek Him.

I have to admit my courtship with God is inconsistent. I pray multiple times a day. I am consistent in my prayer life. I love to sing His praises through songs. Maverick City and Kirk Franklin are the artists I currently frequent. But reading my Bible—not so much. I can find myself getting lost in the stories of the Bible with its intriguing characters and stories of triumph and failure. I can read for hours. But then, I get distracted and may just read one verse the next time I pick up the Bible app or miss days of reading anything. I want to read the Bible in its entirety in this lifetime.

Though the Bible deals with every life issue, most people have never read it, yet it's the blueprint to life that most of us are looking for. When we truly know God for ourselves, we become firm in what we know and don't know. Our faith grows deeper and deeper as we learn more through the scriptures. Man shall not live by bread alone but by every Word that proceeds out of the mouth of God (Matthew 4:4). The Bible is the living Word of God.

Start a different pursuit today.

Prayer: Dear God, please show us how to be in a relationship with you. Let us not get caught up with the customs and traditions of this world, but let us seek you with our whole hearts and find you. Be our strength. Please help us to stand firm in our faith when life is turbulent. Let us dwell in your secret place of protection, love, guidance, and abundance. We love you, Lord. In Jesus's name. Amen.

Reflection: How can you pursue God? Name something new you can try today.

_____

_____

_____

_____

_____

_____

_____

_____

_____

_____

_____

_____

_____

_____

Day 22 in Prayer
Use this section to write down a prayer for today.

_____

_____

_____

_____

_____

_____

_____

_____

_____

_____

_____

_____

_____

_____

_____

_____

DAY

23

FERVENT PRAYER

And he said, "Don't be afraid, Paul, for you will
surely stand trial before Caesar! What's more,
God, in his goodness, has granted safety to
everyone sailing with you." So, take courage!
For I believe God. It will be just as he said.

—ACTS 27:24–25 (NLT)

The *Merriam-Webster Dictionary* defines *fervent* as "exhibiting or marked by great intensity." There will be circumstances in life that require fervent prayer—the kind of prayer that has you wondering if you have prayed enough about a situation. Prayer evolves with such specificity that you find gratitude in your situation.

I recall praying for my husband for months. He was sick, and the doctor could not determine what was wrong. I prayed for discovery, asking the Lord to reveal what was happening in his body to the doctors. All the while, I continued to pray for healing for my husband. One day, the Lord told me to get a second medical opinion. Later that week, I spoke with my mother, who suggested we get a second opinion. I took that to be confirmation. We obtained a second opinion, and the new doctor discovered that my husband had a mass on his colon. If I had not prayed so diligently for him, I do not know how I would have known to change doctors when we did.

When you pray, concentrate on what you're praying for. The scripture says if we believe, we can speak to the mountain, "Move," and it will move (Matthew 17:20 NIV). Believe that God will answer your prayers.

Focusing on God, not the situation, is essential. This requires discretion; be mindful of what you share with others. People mean well, but their perception of the problem, positive or negative, can affect your thoughts and beliefs as well. Know what you know and trust God with the rest.

Reflection: What is the one thing you need to take to God in prayer?

_____

_____

_____

_____

_____

_____

_____

_____

_____

_____

_____

_____

_____

Day 23 in Prayer
Use this section to write down a prayer for today.

DAY

24

We Put Our Faith in God

*Beloved, do not be surprised at the fiery trial when
it comes upon you to test you, as though something
strange were happening to you. But rejoice insofar
as you share Christ's sufferings, that you may also
rejoice and be glad when his glory is revealed.*

—1 PETER 4:12–13 (ESV)

There's a difficult place we find ourselves when we suffer. The *Britannica Dictionary* defines *suffering* as "pain caused by injury, illness, loss, etc.: physical, mental, or emotional pain." As believers in Jesus Christ, we might be inclined to think that we should not suffer. I know that was the case for me for many years. As a Christian, I used to believe my life should be blessed and free from suffering. When difficulties came, I would assume I had done something wrong. I must have sinned or made a poor decision, and now I am dealing with the consequences. But that was not the case.

As I am writing Day 24, I am coming off the tail end of my third pregnancy loss. I had an ectopic pregnancy that eventually began to miscarry naturally. For those of you, readers, who have also experienced this kind of loss, the loss of a pregnancy or child, take care of yourself as you read. If you need to step away from the book to take a break, please do so.

Loss of any kind can be triggering. I share my experience to connect our need for God, Jesus Christ, and prayer in difficult times. Paul says we should not be "surprised" when the trials come. That means we must anticipate that these challenges will come as a means to test us.

Now, let me distinguish one thing. Trials that stretch our faith and trials that come along as a consequence of our choices are different. Some trials are self-inflicted. If you continue to read 1 Peter 4:15, it says, "But let none of you suffer as a murderer or a thief." It means to suffer because of your actions. I make this distinction because we often get into situations that have nothing to do with God. Instead, it was something we wanted or felt we needed, and we suffered the consequences.

What is the proper way to view suffering? I think about how Paul suffered while spreading the good news of Jesus Christ. On the way to Damascus to persecute believers, Paul was blinded during his encounter with Jesus. Once he became a believer, Paul was called to share the Gospel with the Gentiles (non-Jews). Paul's adversaries wanted to kill him, and eventually, he was put in prison. All the while, he persisted in believing that his suffering was for Jesus so that people would believe in Him. He even calls himself "a prisoner of Jesus Christ," noting that he was in bondage for the Savior's sake (Romans 1:1, 1 Corinthians 9:19).

After my miscarriage, the doctor said to me, "This is not your fault." There was nothing I had done to cause this. Instead, the pregnancy started out this way. That statement was comforting. But what comforts me, ultimately, is reminding myself of what God told me. I may not understand the journey and why I have suffered this way, but I know God. I will attach my hope to Him.

Encourage yourself by remembering the previous provisions of God in your life!

Reflection: When challenges arise, what do you tell yourself? How can you challenge that narrative?

_____

_____

_____

_____

_____

_____

_____

_____

_____

_____

_____

_____

_____

_____

_____

Day 24 in Prayer
Use this section to write down a prayer for today.

_____

_____

_____

_____

_____

_____

_____

_____

_____

_____

_____

_____

_____

_____

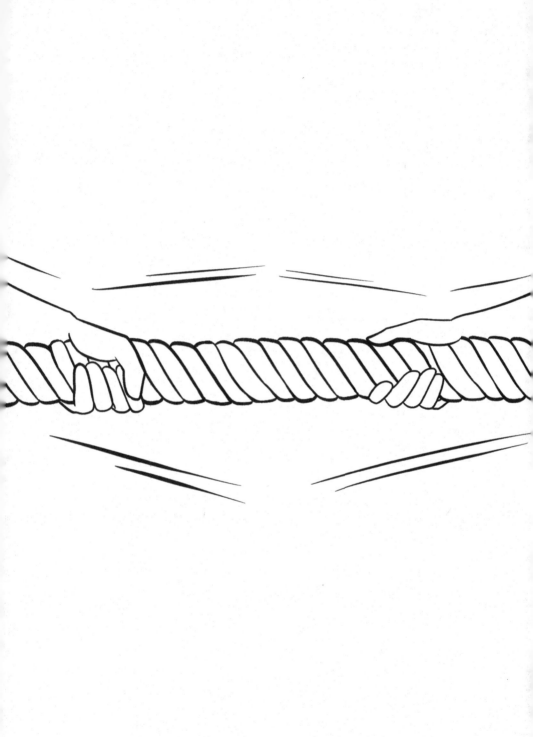

You Don't Need Closure

Then Job replied to the Lord: "I know that you can do all things; no purpose of yours can be thwarted. You asked, 'Who is this that obscures my plans without knowledge?' Surely I spoke of things I did not understand, things too wonderful for me to know."

—JOB 42:1-3 (NIV)

Early one morning, I was in my closet, praying. I was asking God to give me understanding about an incident that happened. He said, "Understanding will not give you peace." I immediately stood up and left the closet. That Word gave me such freedom. The Lord said even if I told you why this happened, you still would not have peace. In this instance, having peace was more important than understanding.

So often, we want closure for situations. We would like to know why the relationship ended. Why did you lose your home? Why did you miss out on that opportunity? Why can't you get pregnant? Why is your child in jail? Why did you get the cancer diagnosis? Why did your parent die? We have to learn to move forward without an explanation.

In the Bible, Job endured tremendous loss. He lost everything: children, wealth, land, animals, and health. His friends attributed this great affliction to God punishing Job. Now we know, as readers, we can peek into this moment when Satan asked for permission to afflict Job to get him to curse God and lose faith. After back-to-back afflictions, Job questioned God about what was happening to him. When God finally answered Job, He did not explain why He lost everything. He doesn't even explain to Job that He was allowing Satan to test him because He trusted Job. Instead, God questions Job about things he said during his distress. Ultimately, God restores Job and gives him double. But God never gave him an explanation.

Are you OK with God not answering your questions? Can you move forward trusting that whatever the reason, God knows what is best for you? We must learn to be content in any state. Otherwise, the pressure can wear us down until we lose faith.

A part of me wants to know why I had four miscarriages. But I know God promised that I would have a son. I would rather not go through the emotional and physical pain of miscarrying. And still, I hold on to the promise of God and release the rest so I do not become bitter and hardened. You do not need closure. You need God's peace that surpasses all understanding. Ask Him to comfort your heart right now.

Reflection: List out the things you want closure for. Pray to God and ask Him to give you peace in these areas.

_____

_____

_____

_____

_____

_____

_____

_____

_____

_____

_____

_____

_____

_____

_____

Day 25 in Prayer

Use this section to write down a prayer for today.

_____

_____

_____

_____

_____

_____

_____

_____

_____

_____

_____

_____

_____

_____

_____

_____

PRAYING FROM A
BROKEN HEART

*Count it all joy, my brothers, when you meet
trials of various kinds, for you know that the
testing of your faith produces steadfastness.*

—JAMES 1:2-3 (ESV)

Sometimes, you get to a place where you must be in or out. Your various commitments, relationships, and responsibilities can be in direct conflict. In the scripture, James tells us to count it all joy when troubles arise. But how often do you look for someone to blame or overanalyze a situation to figure out how you might have avoided it? I have fallen victim to that thinking many times. How arrogant of me to believe that I have that much control over what happens in my life.

Arrogance? Or a misunderstanding of the Christian walk? I've often thought that if I do right by others, seek God in prayer, take care of my responsibilities, be grateful, and work hard, my life should be good. That's only partially true. All things work together for our good! Though "all things" work together, it doesn't mean we won't endure troubles in life. When the trials come, we need to decide what posture to take.

Are you in it for God, trusting that He will see you through anything, or are you out, doubting that God is really there for you because life gets complicated? We cannot be conditional on God. He is gracious and patient with us. But we need to show up for Him even when we do not understand Him. We should love Him unconditionally. God is faithful to complete the good and perfect work He began in you. So, put your faith in God's blessed hope! He will never fail you. Though you may endure, it will strengthen your faith and relationship with God. And honestly, that's worth more than any trial we endure.

Reflection: Looking back over your life, how have trials influenced your faith?

_____

_____

_____

_____

_____

_____

_____

_____

_____

_____

_____

_____

_____

_____

_____

Day 26 in Prayer
Use this section to write down a prayer for today.

_____

_____

_____

_____

_____

_____

_____

_____

_____

_____

_____

_____

_____

_____

_____

_____

Pray in the Silence

*Listen to my Prayer, O God. Do not ignore
my cry for help! Please listen and answer
me, for I am overwhelmed by my troubles.*

—PSALM 55:1–2 (NLT)

David, the man after God's heart, is a solid example of a man of faith. He prayed consistently, trusted God, and obeyed His commands. And yet, when we read the passage in Psalm 55:1, we are left feeling that David longed to hear God's voice. How can the man after God's heart receive silence to his cry for help?

While walking with the Lord, I do not think of silent moments or seasons as God being genuinely silent. I believe He is working and watching. The Bible says God never sleeps or slumbers (Psalm 121:4 NLT). He is divinely orchestrating every situation in the background. Even when we cannot trace God, we can trust He is working. Pray even when you hear nothing back, listen earnestly to a sermon seeking an internal nudge from God, or play your favorite gospel song while looking for a new spiritual encounter. Pray in the silence, assuring yourself that the Lord hears your prayers and is working on it. In due time, He will answer.

Reflection: How do you feel when God seems silent?

_____

_____

_____

_____

_____

_____

_____

_____

_____

_____

_____

_____

_____

_____

Day 27 in Prayer
Use this section to write down a prayer for today.

———————————————————————
———————————————————————
———————————————————————
———————————————————————
———————————————————————
———————————————————————
———————————————————————
———————————————————————
———————————————————————
———————————————————————
———————————————————————
———————————————————————
———————————————————————
———————————————————————
———————————————————————
———————————————————————

I Choose Love

*Three things will last forever—faith, hope,
and love—and the greatest of these is love.*

—1 CORINTHIANS 13:13 (NLT)

*For by that one offering he forever made
perfect those who are being made holy.*

—HEBREWS 10:14 (NLT)

*For God's will was for us to be made
holy by the sacrifice of the body of
Jesus Christ, once for all time.*

—HEBREWS 10:10 (NLT)

Have you heard the saying "Hurt people hurt people"? The sentiment is true in some regard. But I do not particularly care for the adage. People can heal and become better versions of themselves by applying intentionality and effort. The idea that people who are hurting will hurt others insinuates that love is impossible or that somehow hurting others is inevitable. The Bible tells us that love covers a multitude of sins. You can also look at sins as offenses against others.

What we are talking about here is trauma. Trauma results from "exposure to an incident or series of events that are emotionally disturbing or life-threatening with lasting adverse effects on the individual's functioning and mental, physical, social, emotional, and/or spiritual well-being" (Trauma-Informed Care Implementation Resource Center 2023).

Trauma has many forms. We experience trauma as a single event, such as a car accident. We experience trauma repeatedly with exposure to violence or war, for example. We experience trauma after undergoing repeated abuse from another person, and we can experience trauma when a significant loss affects our lives. Regardless of which form has affected you, you can heal through individual work, such as therapy, prayer, and a robust support system. Focusing on God's love for us and our ability to love others is one way to step in the right direction.

You might say, "Audrey, I have never seen love." I submit to you that we can learn how to love. When we read the Bible, we witness how to love in the life of Jesus Christ and countless people in the Old and New Testaments. God is love. We are made in His image. We can learn how to love by being intentional. Love doesn't have to be perfect; it must be genuine and authentic.

Reflection: How do you love? How would your life change if you submitted to love?

_____

_____

_____

_____

_____

_____

_____

_____

_____

_____

_____

_____

_____

_____

_____

Day 28 in Prayer

Use this section to write down a prayer for today.

_____

_____

_____

_____

_____

_____

_____

_____

_____

_____

_____

_____

_____

_____

_____

REMEMBER

*Houses filled with all kinds of good things
you did not provide, wells you did not dig, and
vineyards and olive groves you did not plant—
then when you eat and are satisfied, be careful
that you do not forget the Lord, who brought
you out of Egypt, out of the land of slavery.*

—DEUTERONOMY 6:11–12 (NIV)

When Paul tells us to pray about everything, I think it is more about us learning to surrender to God. He is omniscient. God knows our hearts. He understands what we need. Therefore, our prayers should willingly invite Him into our circumstances, declaring, "Lord, I cannot do this on my own."

To believe Romans 8:28, we must trust God—really trust Him. We talk about believing in God and loving God. But prayer requires us to trust that God will hear and take care of us. Recently, I realized I did not trust God as much as I thought.

I consider myself a "strong" Christian. However, when my husband needed emergency surgery to have a mass removed from his colon, I found myself in a tailspin. I was almost hysterical. I was crying, feeling confused, and trying to make sure I was there for him and taking care of our two young children.

After a day or two, I quickly realized I could not sustain myself in that level of pressure. I had to believe in the God I read about in my Bible. I had to believe in the God I prayed to for countless others to be healed. I had to believe it for myself, and there was no one there to give me a pep talk in the middle of the night as I cried myself to sleep! No, I had to talk to myself aloud until I felt calm enough to move on to the next task. After surgery and eleven days in the hospital, my husband finally came home. That would be the beginning of his journey.

During those days, I remembered all the things God had done for me before. I remembered how He healed my mother of rheumatoid arthritis. I remembered pleading with God for more time after my father suffered a heart attack and a stroke. The Lord gave us nine more years together after that. I remembered God saving our one-week-old daughter when she stopped breathing after choking on milk and had to be rushed to the hospital. The list goes on. My memories are what keeps me. My memories help me stay focused when I want to cry. And I do cry—a lot. But I keep going.

Who have you seen God heal? How has God shown up for the friends and family you love? Remember those things when life gets hard, and you cannot see your way. Remember what God has done. Remember who God is. I assure you, He is not done yet.

Reflection: What has God done for you that you can reflect on? List five things.

_____

_____

_____

_____

_____

_____

_____

_____

_____

_____

_____

_____

_____

_____

_____

Day 29 in Prayer
Use this section to write down a prayer for today.

PRAYING IN HOPE

*May the God of hope fill you with all joy and peace
as you trust in him, so that you may overflow
with hope by the power of the Holy Spirit.*

—ROMANS 15:13 (NIV)

I shared that I believe God for the son He promised me. I am forty-one years old as I am writing this. Sometimes, you must believe God for the impossible—what pastor and author Mike Todd calls crazy faith. I have to believe that what God promised me will come to pass. God does not lie. There is no darkness in Him. What He promises will be fulfilled. I look to the stories of Sarah, Hannah, the Shunammite woman, Rebekah, Elizabeth, and Rachel for encouragement that I will bear a son in due time.

What are you believing God for? A crucial part of faith is discernment. You have to know when to be quiet. Not everyone will have unwavering faith with you. We each have a measure of faith (Romans 12:3). The extent of that faith varies. Listening to the wrong voices can easily deter you, causing you to doubt God. Did God really say that? That is why consistently praying and reading the scriptures are so important. It will help us stand firm in our faith when doubt creeps in. We can discern truth from deception—the difference between right and almost right.

Reflection: What are you hoping for? What do you need from yourself and others while you wait?

_____

_____

_____

_____

_____

_____

_____

_____

_____

_____

_____

_____

_____

_____

Day 30 in Prayer
Use this section to write down a prayer for today.

_____

_____

_____

_____

_____

_____

_____

_____

_____

_____

_____

_____

_____

_____

_____

Letting Go

*Seek his will in all you do, and he will
show you which path to take.*

—PROVERBS 3:6 (NLT)

I expected to be married by the age of twenty-five. When that did not happen, I became antsy. I kept trying to make things work, but my picker was off. I would date these very handsome, successful men, but they all had one thing in common: they were emotionally unavailable. There was always this disconnection at a deeper level. After dating and dating and dating, I finally surrendered to God.

One night, I was alone in my apartment. I prayed something like this: "God, please help me. My picker is off. I cannot find my husband. I am tired of choosing wrong. I surrender. Please have your way. Please prepare me for my husband. Please prepare my husband for me. Let me be ready when he comes. Amen." I prayed this same prayer for about five years.

In March of 2012, my father passed away. As I shared earlier, I was heartbroken. I was comforted by my family and friends. I am so thankful to those who simply sat on the phone while I cried, held me, and checked in on me daily, even when I did not return their text messages or answer their phone calls. They made sure I knew I was not alone.

Later that summer, one of my friends encouraged me to go on a blind date. I did not think anything of it. I had given my will to God, so I was open to meeting someone new. On July 6, 2012, I went on that blind date. Little did I know, that man would be my husband! We got married two years later.

Did you see that? My posture of surrender created room for God to show out when I finally let go. In one of my darkest moments (the mourning of my father's death), God brought light into my life. My husband and I will celebrate ten years of marriage this year. When I speak with friends still waiting to get married, I share how I prayed for my husband. Come to find out he was only one degree of separation from me. We had a mutual friend in common.

As you wait, pray for God to prepare you. It is not about finding a husband or wife but more about being ready when that door opens. Let me also say that not everyone is going to be married. The Bible shows us that. But if that is what God wills for you, I pray that He helps you develop the best parts of yourself while you wait with patience and contentment.

Reflection: What is one aspect of yourself that you want to improve? Remember, it is not about perfection but willingness.

_____

_____

_____

_____

_____

_____

_____

_____

_____

_____

_____

_____

_____

_____

Day 31 in Prayer
Use this section to write down a prayer for today.

_____

_____

_____

_____

_____

_____

_____

_____

_____

_____

_____

_____

_____

_____

_____

_____

BENEDICTION

Devote yourselves to prayer with an alert mind and
a thankful heart.

—Colossians 4:2 (NLT)

Paul often ended his letters in the Bible with a benediction, giving
honor and glory to God while leaving his readers with a charge. See
Ephesians 3:20, Romans 15:13, and 1 Thessalonians 5:23. I thank you
for joining me on this journey of prayer. I pray that God blesses and
rewards your efforts as you strive to draw closer to Him.

"Now to him who is able to keep you from stumbling and to
present you blameless before the presence of his glory with great
joy, to the only God, our Savior, through Jesus Christ our Lord, be
glory, majesty, dominion, and authority, before all time and now and
forever. Amen" (Jude 1:24–25 ESV).

REFERENCES

Britannica Dictionary. "Suffering." Accessed November 1, 2023. https://www.britannica.com/dictionary/suffering

Centers for Disease Control and Prevention. "Rheumatoid Arthritis." Last revised April 7, 2022. https://www.cdc.gov/arthritis/basics/rheumatoid-arthritis.html

Dunham, Lexie, "Burnout vs. Laziness: What's the Difference?" *The Student Movement,* November 10, 2023.

Fenn, Kristina, and Byrne, Majella. "The Key Principles of Cognitive Behavioral Therapy." *InnovAiT,* 6 (9) (September 2013): 579–585. https://doi.org/10.1177/1755738012471029

Jeremiah, David. *The Jeremiah Study Bible: English Standard Version: What it says, what it means, what it means for you.* New York: Worthy Books, 2019.

Life. Church. "Holy Bible." YouVersion, Version 9.33.3 (2001). https://www.youversion.com/the-bible-app/

Merriam-Webster Dictionary. Springfield: Encyclopaedia Britannica, Inc. 2024 https://www.merriam-webster.com/

Mlodinow, Leonard. *Emotional: How Feelings Shape Our Thinking.* New York: Knopf Doubleday Publishing Group, 2022.

Phillips, Anita. *The Garden Within: Where the War with Your Emotions Ends & Your Most Powerful Life Begins.* Nashville: Nelson Books, 2023.

"The Key Principles of Cognitive Behavioural Therapy." *InnovAiT* 6, no. 9 (September 1, 2013): 579–85. https://doi.org/10.1177/1755738012471029.

Trauma-Informed Care Implementation Resource Center. "What is Trauma?" Accessed March 1, 2023. https://www.traumainformedcare.chcs.org/what-is-trauma/

Printed in the United States
by Baker & Taylor Publisher Services